WordPress Website Security Guide

Disclaimer: Every effort has been made to that WordPress Website Security Guide provides as accurate information as possible.

However, sometimes, errors do happen, and the author does not claim that the information is accurate. Several software tools are recommended throughout the WordPress Website Security Guide, but the author is not the developer or the owner of these scripts and makes no claim to the functionality of them.

Contents

Introduction

Humans naturally take security very seriously in their personal lives.

For example, before you go to bed, you make sure to lock the doors and shut and secure the windows. You make sure to keep track of where your keys for your home, motor vehicle, or other valuable items are at. You keep your credit cards, driver's license, and other personal identification items sheathed in a wallet or purse. However, you may also know that having one layer of protection is not enough. For example, instead of having one regular lock for your door you may have a regular lock with the addition of deadbolt lock, just in case one key gets lost your house is still safe from intruders. The same philosophy should be applied to your WordPress powered website. WordPress is an amazing open-source technology with a sizable community of users that contribute to it. However, there is also a

community of pernicious users that want to destroy your site and everything you worked for. Use the methods taught in this product to crystallize your WordPress site so that it will be as tough to break as a rock.

1: First Things First

Question: A security vulnerability in any of the following devices could cause your WordPress site to get hacked.

1. Your local machine
2. A device that assists in keeping your server up and running
3. A commercial plugin that you purchased from an online vendor

The ANSWER: All of the above! I know this is surprising to some but keep this in mind, your WordPress site is only as strong as your weakest link.

If a hacker seizes your WordPress login credentials from a file called "WordPress_password.txt" that's sitting on the Desktop of your Dell

[3]

laptop, then they can easily hack into your site. If a hacker is listening to your instant message conversation that you are having with your WordPress tech guy and see you send them your login credentials, then they could intercept your message and break into your WordPress site.

The list of possible attacks is very extensive, so that's why I'm going to explain the most common ones. However, before we proceed, let me make one thing crystal clear to you; there is no instant method to securing your site.

If more than one person knows your WordPress administration details, then that's a loophole you have in your website's security.

If you install source code without understanding it then that is a security outlet. The risks are always there, but that's why I must help you understand them and to protect your site from them as much as possible.

Common security threats

Computer virus:

This is one of the most commonly known and confused threats. A computer virus is a program that can reproduce itself and spread across other computers. Ways that you can obtain a computer virus is by:

1. Downloading corrupted files from the internet, i.e., dreggy applications from torrent sites

2. Visiting corrupted sites that automatically download the harmful source code to your browser
3. External storage devices that contain bad files (i.e., USB stick or hard drive)

Computer viruses are commonly erringly used to refer to other types of malware such as spyware, computer worms, and Trojan horses.

Computer Worm:

Commonly referred to as a worm, is a form of malware that causes harm to your computer by duplicating itself so that it can contaminate other computers. They usually have prodigious success by replicating itself across a network and accomplish this by abusing security weaknesses. Compared to viruses, worms do not attach themselves to the existing source code but are standalone programs that usually cause some harm to the network even if it's just gobbling up bandwidth.

Spyware:

This is a type of malware that collects information about an individual's browsing habits without their knowledge.

The practicality of spyware is often a controversial argument.

Some employers may implement spyware (key loggers) to track employee's computer activity and measure how productive they are at work. Devious users may use spyware to snatch an individual's keyboarding habits so that they can rift into their Facebook account. Online merchants like Amazon may use cookies which are technically spyware for marketing purposes.

Rootkit:

This is a sneaky snake of malware. It pretends to be a helpful program but cloaks malicious programs so that antivirus (AV) software can't detect it. The term rootkit is an amalgamation of root and kit. Root is the administrative user in a UNIX system, while kit is the component of a program that implements the tool.

Key loggers:

Also referred to as keystroke logging, is the method of recording the activity on a keyboard. This is usually done clandestinely so that the individual is unaware that their privacy is being violated. Key loggers come in various shapes and forms. They can capture instant messaging, text messaging, phone numbers, and even record your actions from your desktop by using your webcam!

Trojan Horse:

The devil in disguise. This is a computer program that masquerades as a friendly one, but is actually malicious and will cause bodily harm to your computer by allowing the hacker access to it.

Blended threats: Most of the threats these days are a deadly, poisonous, concentration of multiple doses of loathsome malware. For example, a threat containing a Trojan horse, worm, and spyware may attempt to penetrate the defenses of your computer system.

Buffer overflow attacks

A buffer overflow results from an error in the source code. This is why it's so crucial that you only install plugins from sources that use quality assurance measures to make sure that their code is safe for your site. What happens is while the program is writing data to the buffer (memory), the memory is overloaded. Buffer

[11]

overflows are common in languages in which the programmer manages memory, and is a common exploit in web forms.

A way that programmers can check to ensure that their program does not allow for the buffer to happen is to make sure that they do the proper bounds checking.

Brute force attack

This is a type of cryptanalytic attack that decodes passwords by doing exhaustive trial and errors. If you ever have seen a movie that involves highly secretive information, then you may see a "hacker" sitting down on some executive's computer desk and repeatedly entering in passwords until they magically guess the correct one.

Well, I'm sure that you figure out a long time ago that movies are just a wee bit dramatized, but this is in essence what a computer program does during a brute force attack. Computers are a whole lot more efficient in doing data crunching than humans so a hacker could run a brute force script on your wp-admin directory and crack your WordPress site. They could then proceed to post embarrassing/obscene content using your name and your site, which could destroy your reputation in the blogosphere. No worries, I show how you can easily protect your administrative password from being cracked by these attacks in the future sections.

Cross-site scripting (XSS)

This is a type of vulnerability that is a mixture of poorly coded software and an unsecured site. This attack allows hackers to insert client-side scripts like JavaScript into web pages that users utilize, which is then downloaded to the host's computer and infects them locally.

According to Symantec, cross-site scripting is responsible for most of the security vulnerabilities. Below is an illustrational example of a common XSS attack which uses an iframe. I will be using the classical stock characters from computer security.

1. Alice is visiting a university portal which is hosted on the XYZ server. She logs in with her username/password which stores private data such as address and billing information.
2. Trudy realizes that XYZ server is vulnerable to XSS.
3. Naughty Trudy develops a deceptive URL that will exploit the vulnerability to the fullest, and emails, Alice, pretending to be a representative from her University that encourages her to update her password because their university's server has recently been exploited. The link will aim to XYZ's server through an iframe but will contain Trudy's malicious code.
4. Alice makes the costly mistake of visiting Trudy's URL while logged into the site hosted on XYZ server.

[15]

5. Trudy's malicious code runs in Alice's browser as if it came from XYZ server. Trudy then uses the script to steal Alice's cookie session and steals her credit card information.

This chapter hopefully refreshed and also extended your knowledge about the common computer security threats. I would highly recommend staying up to date with the latest threats because they are never-ending. I would recommend following this website to see the latest malware threats: http://www.symantec.com/security_response/. The more you can stay up with them, the better you will be prepared for them.

2: Webhosting

Having a secured server is an acutely important aspect of WordPress security, but depending on what type of hosting plan you're using this may be out of your control. For example, if you are using dedicated hosting, then you are the server administrator and have complete control over what you do and do not install.

However, if you are using a shared web host, then not only do you have little control over the server, but you are also sharing the same server with 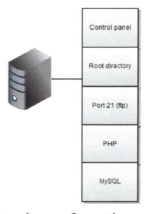 a potential of hundreds of other webmasters! Let me illustrate some technologies that an example server may have.

Just think of your server as a dresser or a chest of drawers. You may have t-shirts, undergarments, socks, and pajamas in separate departments. If it's a solid dresser, then each chest should have their separate department, and all of your belongings are secured.

However, if the dresser is old and deteriorated, then it may be missing some chests. If it's missing one, then this means that through any abandoned space you should be able to prop open other closed chests.

This is a vivid example that illustrates the vulnerabilities that typical web servers face daily. Any unsecured port on your server is security vulnerability and will allow a hacker to access other parts of your server. All it takes is one weakness.

Password Enigma

Make sure that you devise long-winded elaborate passwords that you can remember. Avoid using dictionary names and meeting the minimum requirements of password lengths. Just keep in mind that every character you add to your password will increase the complexity for hackers to break it by magnitudes.

For example, if your password is just three characters long and you're using characters from the English alphabet, then your password will take 26^3 = 17,576 permutations to decode which is something that a computer with minimal processing power can crack in short time duration.

The mathematics behind this is that there are 26 characters in the English alphabet and that out of a password with a length of three there are 26*26*26 total unique possibilities as illustrated

in the diagram

26	26	26

However, if you increase the length of the password by just one character, then you'll have 26^4= 456,976 possibilities that

vou can choose from.

As you can see, increasing your password length by just one character makes it significantly more difficult to crack. Other ways that you can increase your password security is by throwing in a combination of uppercase letters and non-alphanumeric characters.

Examples of non-alphanumeric characters are anything that's not a letter or a number such as: [, %,^,&,}, ~,

/, *, @, etc.

Password management

One of the highest reviewed and recommended password tools is called LastPass, which is free to download. The fact of the matter is if you have used the Internet for more than a year, then you already have more accounts than you can remember. You probably at least have two of the following:

- Social network profile
- Email account
- Forum account

If you are security savvy, then you probably do not use the same username and password for each network as not only can hackers trace your digital footprints, but they can also find out more about you just from navigating the sites that you visit. The more activity you display on the internet means, the easier it is to extract data about you.

[21]

For example, let's say that a hacker can track the digital footprints that Bob takes. Bob may wonder why anyone would care about the hours he spends daily FIFA forums, the love he confesses for Laure Boulleau on his blog, and the money he spends on signed memorabilia from his favorite players.

Well, believe it, or not, this information can be very handy to a hacker. For one, they will be able to track the real Bob Smith on Facebook, as I imagine that there are thousands of them on there. He could then pose as a faux representative for Ms. Boulleau to extort sensitive data like credit card information. Sorry, Bob, Ms. Boulleau was not interested in meeting you in Europe, that hacker just wanted your credit card information so that they too can purchase signed soccer memorabilia!

Hopefully, this colorful example would convince you that a secured password manger is a way to go. The good thing about LastPass is that its hyper secured as its using AES encryption which has been established by the United States government (NIST).

If it's good enough to be used by the US government, then I think it's safe to say that you can try it without being paranoid. Also, all your encryption/decryption is done locally so that it never travels across the internet.

Encryption is the process in which data is transferred into gibberish, and decryption is the process of converting gibberish back to the actual password. For example, the password"testing123" is **encrypted** to "35%^nj78J8jm"hI0, and the password "Hssh6&*IIJS^&jsnsnsmm867gs" is **decrypted** to "howtheheckthishappen?"

Below are illustrational examples for the encryption and decryption mechanism:

Encryption:

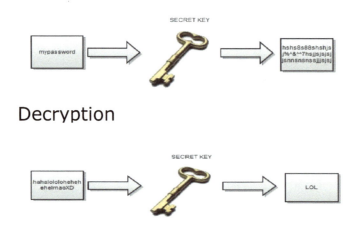

Decryption

Only the encrypted passwords are stored on their secured servers, and let's say that in the worst-case scenario a hacker does access the servers, they will still have their work cut out because the only thing they will have access to is the encrypted files, aka the gibberish.

Here is the download URL for LastPass: https://lastpass.com/.

[24]

The installation instructions for this program are very easy. The program and run the executable file. While running the program, you should see a dialog box that gives you three opinions. You can make a LastPass account, already have one, or skip importing passwords and data as indicated in the screenshot below.

After you make your account and enter in your password, they will ask you to reenter it. Just to clarify this is the master password and it should be high security. Also, you should not forget it!

I wouldn't recommend saving it in a text file on your computer or less you put it in an odd location and encrypt it with a strong key. The easiest route is to write it down and put it somewhere safe, like in a safe box!

After that is done, the installer will ask you if you want to import any data into LastPass. Select whichever option you fancy.

[26]

After that is done, the installer will ask you if you want to stay logged into LastPass, or if you prefer to be automatically logged out once your browser closes. If you're not paranoid, choose
the first option, if you want to have an easier time sleeping at night then select the second.

Utilizing LastPass

Using LastPass is very simple. I have LastPass installed on Google Chrome and have highlighted the icon for you below in red so that you can see how it looks.

Other than that everything for this application is pretty self-explanatory. Just navigate across the web, and

[27]

whenever you want to create an online account somewhere just fill in the form and LastPass volunteers to save this data so that next time you won't have to go through the process again.

Additional Security

With all the technological advances these days, you can never be too safe. If you feel like your master password is not enough protection, then you can always add additional layers of security to your LastPass account. To do this, visit your LastPass account and login here: https://lastpass.com.

Once logged in, click on settings, security, and you should be redirected to a graphical user interface with several options. The default security level is normal, but if you want to amp it up then select either medium-high or high. Also, there is a nifty feature called the *Grid Multifactor Authentication* that I would highly recommend taking advantage of.

This allows a user to authenticate by using the common name/password pair with an additional passcode that is supplied by the grid that you can print and keep in a secured location, so not on your desk, or underneath your bed!

This means that if a hacker somehow gets your username and password, they will still need the secret passcode to successfully authenticate into your LastPass account!
Here is an example of what the

grid looks like:

	A	B	C	D	E	F	G	H	I	J	K	L	M	N	O	P	Q	R	S	T	U	V	W	X	Y	Z	
0	h	i	h	v	k	g	z	u	v	p	5	i	g	b	k	e	a	e	k	t	i	f	d	6	p	6	0
1	x	6	2	s	c	b	2	j	w	d	r	p	y	e	4	u	n	c	v	y	g	w	5	s	g	e	1
2	y	k	c	e	i	z	c	b	i	e	c	c	q	z	g	7	f	6	d	b	r	s	d	e	h	k	2
3	3	e	5	b	i	u	n	k	z	w	d	3	x	n	7	z	q	p	s	x	n	x	u	r	y	d	3
4	a	4	i	i	f	d	n	b	e	x	v	s	b	n	f	e	g	5	s	f	w	a	u	f	x	9	4
5	5	i	r	u	n	r	p	w	2	v	2	g	w	6	5	j	q	6	y	w	c	6	s	u	c	g	5
6	v	x	m	j	w	h	u	f	4	9	x	j	w	q	6	p	x	u	m	t	6	4	r	v	r	t	6
7	s	b	f	v	h	2	j	u	c	9	4	w	e	x	w	3	9	k	j	6	z	9	r	e	t	n	7
8	9	b	b	r	v	u	s	2	g	z	t	s	m	v	r	g	j	w	5	9	r	5	j	3	2	c	8
9	2	i	h	m	x	g	n	z	x	b	k	g	3	s	9	m	c	k	a	t	s	k	h	p	j	y	9
	A	B	C	D	E	F	G	H	I	J	K	L	M	N	O	P	Q	R	S	T	U	V	W	X	Y	Z	

LastPass may ask you to enter in your pass code for the combination N9 Q2 Z5 which would translate to "sfg."

If you're super paranoid, then you can consider getting some biometric action going on and purchasing a fingerprint or card reader authentication device.

Here is a USB one that you can get on Amazon:

https://www.amazon.com/Fingerprint
-PQI-Matching-Biometric-
Security/dp/B06XG4MHFJ/ref=sr_1_1
_sspa?keywords=Fingerprint+usb&qi
d=1563521928&s=gateway&sr=8-1-
spons&psc=1

This is the equivalent of one of those spy films in which the secret agent puts his hand through a mechanical device that verifies his identity by DNA typing, and then authenticates him through a secret door. Well, not precisely that intricate but I think you get the point.

3: Windows Guardianship

Windows have a swell feature that allows individuals to securely backup their most precious files just in case a disaster happens. The first step is to go to your control panel, which you can get there by clicking on Start ->control panel, and then clicking on "Backup your computer."

You should see a dialog box that looks like the screenshot below.

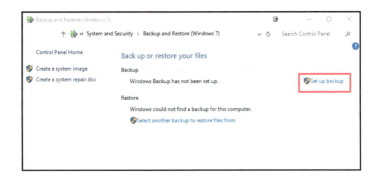

You will then have the option to let windows select which file to backup,

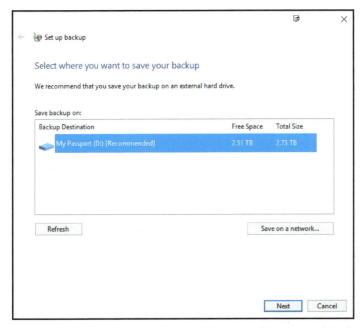

Or you can personally select which files you want, the choice is entirely up to you.

I decided that for today only I will be complacent and choose the default option. Next, you will see a list of files that Windows will backup and where exactly they will back up this data to indicated in the screenshot below:

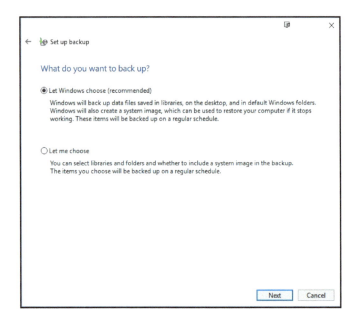

Once you do that you should see a dialog box that asks you where you want to backup your data to. If you're okay with everything, then *click save settings and run my backup*. You should then see a progress bar that tells you how much remaining time you have until the backup is completed as indicated in the screenshot below:

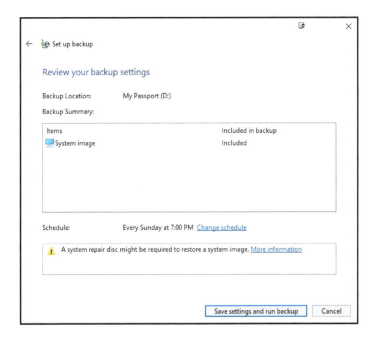

That's all there is to perform a backup. What I will show you next is

Media	Pros	Cons
Internal hard drive	• Fast • Don't take up any ports on your computer like the USB drive • Easy to carry since it's located inside your computer • Is disaster proof as they can be easily ported into a	• Need to be knowledgeable with computers in order to remove the case and insert the hard drive inside • Can't be used on other computers easily since it's located inside your computer • Limited in

a list of media to copy your files to.

[35]

		unplug and scuttle
USB	• Small and easy to carry • Portable • Good for storing small files • Economical in the short run	• Space limitations • Relatively expensive
Writeable CDs	• Good for small backups • Portable • Easy to store • Inexpensive • Easy to purchase. Modern electronic or convenient stores should hold them	• Small disk space. The average space it can hold is 740 MB • Not all computers have CD burners • Easily scratched and damaged • Don't always burn correctly • Slow
	• Can store large amounts of	• Not all computers

	new machine	storage capacity depending on the model of your computer
External hard drive	• Easy to use • Can store lots of data • Portable • Compatible with many operating systems • Can be used on multiple computers • Scalable. Once you run out of space just get another one	• Can be relatively expensive as they are not the cheapest media in terms of per gigabyte storage • Slow compared to an internal hard drive because a USB connection is not as efficient as an internal connection • Bad logistics. It will make the office more cluttered, or will require you to carry more equipment • Security. Someone can

Writeable DVDs	data	have DVD burners
File sharing network	• Economical • High data retention • Portable • Easy to purchase	• Easily scratched
Network Attached Storage (NAS)	• Your own personal cloud • No monthly fees • Stores a lot of data • Can access it anywhere • Economical	• Security threats • Difficult to troubleshoot

How to find compatible internal hard drives:

The first thing you need to do is find the specifications of your hard drive. You can do this by searching_online for the model of the computer you are using. Or, you can easily do this in Windows 10 by following these steps:

Step One:

Click on the Windows icon (located in the bottom left-hand corner of your screen)

Step Two:

Right-click on "Window Icon" and then select "Computer Management" as indicated in the screenshot below. in the screenshot below.

Apps and Features

Mobility Center

Power Options

Event Viewer

System

Device Manager

Network Connections

Disk Management

Computer Management

Windows PowerShell

Windows PowerShell (Admin)

Task Manager

Settings

File Explorer

Search

Run

Shut down or sign out

Desktop

Type here to search

Step Three:

Click on "Storage" and then click the Arrow icon underneath "Disk

[39]

Management" as indicated in the

screenshot below:

Congratulations, now you have found the model number of the hard drive you are using.

You can simply input this number into Google to find compatible hard drives. You can use any of the following:

- External hard drive
- USB stick
- Network Attached Storage
- CD-R/DVD+R,
- Secure Cloud Storage

[40]

4: The One Minute Fix to Hardening Windows

Note: The process in Windows 10 is more or less similar.

There is one utility on Microsoft Windows that the average user seldom uses, and that's called *Microsoft System Configuration Utility*, colloquially known as Msconfig. This is a tool that is normally used for troubleshooting system issues as it allows administrators to disable the software and device drivers. However, what the average window 10 user doesn't know is that it can also be used for hardening the security of your machine. Allow me to show you the quick and easy steps that you can take to make your computer more secured.

[41]

Step One

Click on the windows start button located in the left-hand corner of your screen as indicated in the screenshot below.

Step Two

Type in "MSConfig" into the search form as indicated in the screenshot below.

A tabulated dialog box should promptly appear. Click on the Tools tab, select click the "Change UAC Settings," and then click the launch button as indicated in the screenshot below.

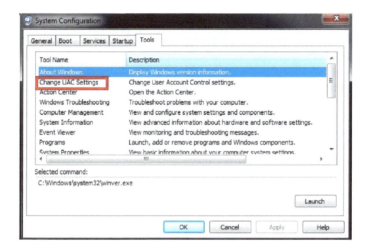

Now you can amp up the security of
your windows 10 operating system by
scrolling up.

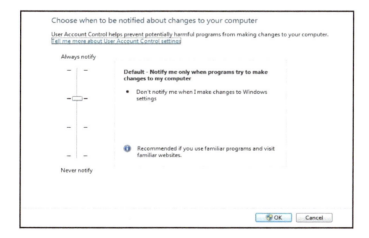

[43]

Just to let you know, enabling this tends to slow down the installation of software programs. If you want my advice that I would like to consider credible, while you are installing the software, you can disable this, and the enable this once the software is installed. However, if you are a paranoid parrot, then you can keep your system on maximum security watch the entire time.

5: Inside the mind of a Professional Hacker

Have you ever seen a crime movie? If you did, then you may remember seeing a detector thinking like a criminal, which is a proven way to track and stop them. Believe or not this is the similar frame of mind that you need to get in if you plan on stopping hackers. You need to start thinking like one! Below are the common steps that a hacker will take when they try to penetrate the defenses of your internet business.

Step One: Data analysis

In this step, the hacker collects information about the host, such as the web technologies they have installed on their server. They do this by being very subtle such as looking at the cache of the site so that the

[45]

webmaster will not be able to see any paper trail in their web analysis tools.

They could also use other various means like social engineering to pry out the details from your hands without you expecting anything suspicious. Social engineering is, in essence, an elaborate lie that is hard to detect because the hacker built the lie off accurate details. Let's say that you made a recent purchase of something and disposed of the receipt.

The hacker could engage in what's known as *dumpster diving* to obtain the receipt of your recent electronic purchase. They could then find your email details on a forum or by messaging you on Facebook about something that you'll be interested in.

Since they have already built up a decent amount of data about you, they could then send you an authoritative email from the company you recently purchased from asking you to purchase additional complimentary items at an extraordinary discount, or they could ask you to update your payment details and provide you a reason for doing so. As you can see, social engineering has very little to do with computer skills, but more to do with being a deceptive jerk. One of the most notorious hackers Kevin Mitnick, was an expert at this. The good news for him is that he turned a new leaf and is no longer engaging in such acts, or so we are told. Having a cache of

your website doesn't serve you any search engine benefits, and it allows hackers to do some private investigation on your website, so I would recommend removing these pages from the Google index. To learn how to remove cache pages from Google, go to https://www.google.com/webmasters/tools/removals?pli=1

Step Two: Investigation

Kind of like how authorities investigate into a crime by asking questions, searching through documents, and confiscating suspected person's belongings, a hacker does something similar in this stage. They use data mining by executing queries that will provide them info that they are seeking. They may also search the server looking for any potential security leaks. This is another good reason for you to be constantly monitoring your web stats for how visitors are finding your sites, and what search queries they are using to get there. Popular analytic tools include the forever popular Google analytics, and also Piwik, which is the most popular open-source web analytics software on the market.

Both of these tools allow you to find search queries that individuals are using on your site.

Escalating Access

Once the hacker has entered your system, they can look for gaps in your configuration and exploit it to the fullest. For example, they can bypass restrictions and allow themselves to become an administrator. If a hacker can accomplish this, then all bets are off, and your site is at the boon of the hacker. Experienced hackers will usually "keep the door to your site propped open" via a rootkit before diving into other areas of the server. If the hacker is seasoned, then they would modify the log files so that their activity will not be detected.

The source code

Hackers like to view your source code for what programming languages are being used, hidden fields, and HTML comments.

Even though I'm a massive advocate of the well-documented source code,
I do not recommend having your comments viewable to the public. I would recommend asking your programmer to make a separate word document that describes the variables, and functions or methods that are used, and to keep this file in a secure location. Having good comments will only make it easier for hackers to understand and reverse engineer your source code.

Below are several tools that hackers utilize to find out more information about your site. My recommendation is to use these sites for potential data that you do not want to be exposed, and then remove it from your website. If these sites keep a cached version of your data then politely email them asking to remove it from their database.

About us: http://www.aboutus.org/	This is a metasearch engine That collects information about sites from several sources and then combines them in one organized fashion. Even though this is a useful marketing tool, this means that if these devices get in the hands of unethical users, then bad things can happen!
Alexa: http://www.alexa.com/	This is one of the leading web analytics software on the web and provides tremendous information about sites indexed in its database.
Facebook:	It's okay to network and meet

https://www.facebook.com/	New people, but perhaps you shouldn't be telling everybody too much about your interests. For example, if I'm a geek and love computers, then I shouldn't be too specific about my interests because this could be content that a spammer uses to crack into one of my sites.
Linkedin: http://www.linkedin.com/	Often contains work history about an individual such as resumes.
Pipl: https://pipl.com/	This will provide you a digital footprint of an individual's professional and social endeavors.
Twitter: www.twitter.com	Individuals express opinionated thoughts or provide the web with their current activities.
Who.is: http://who.is/	This provides a multitude of

	analytic details of a site such as estimated traffic stats, IP address, name servers, and domain name registration/ renewal dates.

So now that we have figured out the steps that a typical hacker follow to crack sites, let's learn how to become a hacker ourselves so that we can prevent our websites from becoming helpless targets.

Google Hacked!

We all know that search engines allow anyone with an internet connection, the ability to data-mine for content efficiently, and when it comes to search engines, Google is the king. Since Google is the most popular search engine, you can bet that hackers are putting Google number one on its priority list for sites to use to extort security vulnerabilities from sites. However, contrary to popular belief, data mining from Google is not as black or white as running a couple of keyword searches for a domain name.

Hackers typically use an operator with the conjunction of several search queries to process how Google should show its input.

An example of search input that a hacker may use is:

Operator:keyword1 keyword2 keyword3 keyword4... keywords (n denotes an arbitrary variable).

Here are a couple of key factors you should note when doing advance searches in Google. The first is that there is no space between the operator and the first keyword. If you put a space there, then your search results will be dramatically skewed. Also, operators are sensitive since using site:www.xyz.com will generate different results from SITE:www.xyz.com. I would always recommend using lower case operators as they produce more accurate results.

One of the most used operators

The most commonly used operator by far is the "site" operator.

You have probably learned about this operator in the first course you took about search engine optimization. The operator works like this:

site:www.websiteurl.com

This operator returns the pages of a site that are indexed in Google. However, what you were probably not told is that hackers also make use of this operator to learn more about your site. They can use it to reverse engineer your file structures or to find the URLs of certain web pages that they want to look at via cache so that here will be no paper trail. To look at the cache version of a website or webpage, use this operator: cache:www.websiteurl.com.

However, if a webmaster has a site with many pages like a forum, for example, then a hacker may filter down the results by using multiple keywords.

For example, if an individual has a forum about video games, then a search query that a hacker may use is something like this:

```
site:www.xyzsite.com xbox360
first person shooters
```

What this search query may return are discussions about Xbox 360 first person shooting games. However, there is more they can do to refine the search results.

They can slightly modify the previous search query to state something like this:

```
site:www.xyzsite.com "fourth
quarter" xbox360 first person
shooters
```

As you can see, I introduced some additional text that is encapsulated within quotations. Whenever you add quotation marks around text, then it includes the exact phrase. So the format is operator: phrase keyword1 keyword2.

Moving along another commonly used operator is a link. Below is an example of how you can use it:

link:www.xyz.com

Just like with the "site" operator, you do not include any space between the operator and the colon. What this does is provides the inbound links to a URL.

Keep in mind that Google does not provide all the links to a particular URL, as this would provide seasoned search engine professionals with more insights into how their search engine algorithm functions.

Scanning a website for certain files

Hackers love searching websites for files because the more technical data they extract, the easier their job is. Here is an example query that scans a website for it's *about* page:

site:www.xyz.com about.html

If this query doesn't provide you with an about page, then it's more than likely that a company used a different URL for it such as aboutus.html or even history.html.

The search query will at a minimum return back URLs from that site that contains the chosen keywords. What type of data is the following search query trying to extract?

```
site:www.xyz.com          filetype:xls
"customers emails phone numbers."
```

As you may have been able to deduct from hypothetical analysis, the following query extracts a site for an excel file that contains their customer names, emails, and phone numbers. Below is an alphabetical list of file types listed in Google.

Excel (.xls, .xlsx)

Flash (.swf)
HTML (.htm, .html)

Java (.java)
PDF (.pdf)

Perl (.pl)

Make sure to experiment and search queries across your site to see if there are any sensitive data that you have floating around. Remember, to stop hackers; you must first think like one.

Maltego

If you're new to this security game, then it may be hard to think about all possible threats. So what's the solution? Well, like with many technical issues, you can always use good ole software to help troubleshoot certain issues that you may run into.

Software that I highly recommend is Maltego - https://www.maltego.com/. You have the option of purchasing either a commercial copy or using the free one. As with most software that uses this model the free software will be missing certain features that is only available in the paid solution, but if you're new to security management, then you don't need to worry about this in the beginning.

The software is compatible in all major operating systems,Windows, Apple, and Linux so there shouldn't be much of a limitation to get you up and to run. Also the software is very easy to install as if you're using Windows you can simply download and run the software on your computer.

This software gathers and analyzes data related to security issues. This is useful because it saves you time on where to start. Below is a screenshot of the software in action.

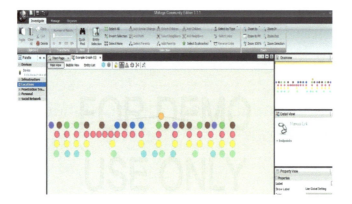

Penetration Testing

This is for the bold and courageous. If you like what you read thus far and want to take your security knowledge to the next level, then what better way to do it then to conduct live examples? One way that you can ethically penetrate a network infrastructure is by using a virtual machine testing tool known as Back Box. You can visit the website here: http://www.backbox.org/. It contains a myriad of software tools such as:
- Network analysis
- Stress tests
- Sniffing tests
- Vulnerability assessments
- Computer forensics

If this is too geeky for you, no worries, things will get better.

6: WordPress Insurance:Raze your WordPress Admin Account

The very first thing you should do in your WordPress account is to eradicate your admin username. Before WordPress 3, the admin account was automatically made by default.

The problem with admin is that hackers know that many WordPress administrators are keeping it as their default username. If they know the path to your WordPress login (which is not hard if you didn't change it), and if they know that you are using admin as your username, then all they have to do is use a software program that computes the brute force algorithm to crack into your WordPress administrator site.

Once they are in there, then all bets are off, and they have full control of your WordPress blog. Below is an illustrational example of the typical file structure of a WordPress site installed on a subdomain.

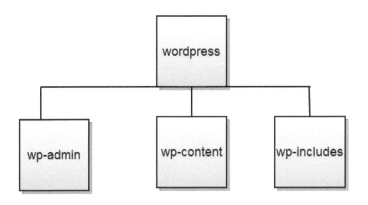

The root folder to the WordPress site is WordPress, and its subdirectories or children are wp-admin, wp-content, and wp-includes. Directories are Linux version of folders. For example, a folder on your Windows desktop is the equivalent to a directory on a Linux machine. Just like the folder holds files, images, content, etc., the same concept applies for directories on your WebHost.

If you were to navigate into these files, then you should see a mixture of PHP, CSS, images, and JavaScript files. So since the organizational architecture of WordPress is made known to the entire internet, this means that hackers have documentation to study so that they crack WordPress systems.

For example, let's say that your domain name is ilovegoogle.com.

The path to your WordPress administrative login is ilovegoogle.com/WordPress/wp-admin.

All the hacker needs to do is utilize a brute force script to crack into your WordPress administrative site. So, let's figure out some simple ways that we can combat this vulnerability.

How to change your admin username

Once you are logged into your WordPress dashboard, click on "Users" and then select "Add New" as indicated in the screenshot below.

From there enter the new information for your new admin, and make sure to give them administrative rights as shown in the screenshot below.

Click "Add New User," and it should be added. Only after your new user is

added should you try and delete your original one. You can do this in the same section you added the new delete as indicated in the screenshot below.
User.

View all users, select the "admin" username, and then select Depending on several variables you may or may not be able to delete your original administrative account, but that's not an issue because you can do that via phpMyAdmin. You can get there by logging into your control panel and clicking on the icon which is indicated in the screenshot below.

and then clicks on the "wp_users" to see the list of users that you have on your website.

From there, select the user that you want to delete and then click the delete link as an in the screenshot below.

You should see a dialog box that confirms the deletion of the user.

Click Ok to confirm this as indicated in the screenshot below. The user should now no longer be there as shown in the screenshot below.

Destroy the README File

The readme file is a file that is typically distributed with computer software that provides information about files in the software, and other useful data such as features and installation instructions. Even though this may sound good on paper, this is a security vulnerability because WordPress tells you what version number you are using in this text file. The good news is it is extremely easy to get rid of it. Simply log in to your FTP software and visit this path on your server: public_html/blog/readme.html. Note that blog denotes the directory in which WordPress is installed on your server. The readme file should show a page that looks like the screenshot below:

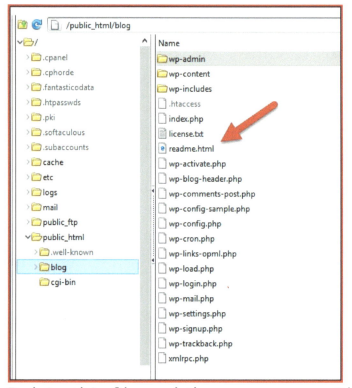

Delete this file and then move on with this information product. Keep in mind that every time you update WordPress, you should execute this procedure again because a new readme file will be created in its honor.

Change the WordPress tables prefix

The WordPress database, like many open source content management projects, comprises of a never-ending amount of tables. Also, there is something about these tables that they have in common. Take a look at the latest version of WordPress tables:

- wp_commentmeta
- wp_comments
- wp_links
- wp_options
- wp_postmeta
- wp_terms
- wp_term_relationships
- wp_term_taxonomy
- wp_usermeta
- wp_users

Do you see something that all of them have in common? They all start with the prefix wp_. This is a security

[73]

leak because if any of these tables have a vulnerability that needs to be patched, then a hacker can use a SQL injection to exploit it. To prevent this from happening, you can manually change the name of your databases. I would recommend trying the manual approach first because if you mess something up, then at least you know the last thing you did. If you're using a plugin and it stops prematurely, then you have no idea where the program ended and you will be left bewildered. However, before you use any approach, it's a must that you first backup your WordPress database.

How to backup your database in Cpanel

Once logged into cPanel scroll down to where you see databases and click on the phpMyAdmin icon as highlighted in the screenshot below.

View your databases on the left-hand column of the screen and click the database that was used to create your WordPress site. Next, click on "Export" shown below.

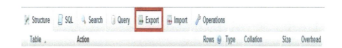

Keep the format as SQL and then click the go button.

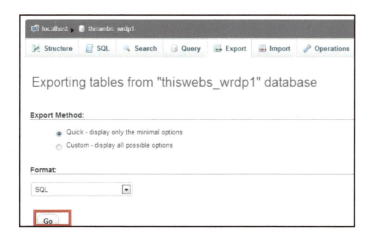

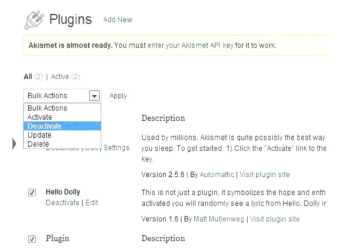

Congratulations, you have just backed up your WordPress blog database. Make sure to save it to a location in which you can easily retrieve.

Deactivate your WordPress plugins

It's a good idea to temporarily deactivate your WordPress plugins before you change the prefix of your WordPress tables. To do this, log into your WordPress dashboard, click on plugins, highlight the plugins that you want to deactivate, select deactivate from bulk actions, and then click apply as indicated in the screenshot below.

Replace your table prefixes

You can use notepad if you're on Windows or Text Edit on OS X for your text editor. If you're on Windows, I will highly recommend using Notepad++ as it has many more features than the default text editor of notepad.

Once your SQL file is opened in your text editor, use the search and replace feature to replace all of the "wp_" prefixes. The short cut for search and replace is "ctr+f," and then click on the "Find in Files" tab.

The new prefix of your WordPress tables should be complicated just like your passwords so that it will be difficult for hackers to crack. A prefix of "thisisnoteasytocrack_" is better than wp_, but GHSbs6ks982ggh_ is much better.

So, make a complicated database prefix and then replace it with the default prefix of wp_. You should get a dialog box that says that you are going to replace 64 occurrences as indicated in the screenshot below.

Drop your tables

Log into phpMyAdmin, and click on the database that you want to drop. Highlight all of the tables, click the "With selected" dialog box, and the n select drop as indicated in the screenshot below.

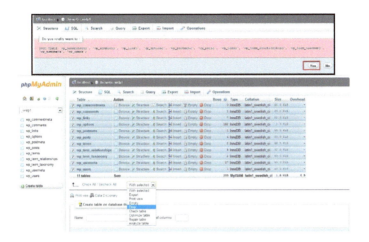

Upon doing so, it will ask you for confirmation if you want to delete the tables. Click the Yes button.

You should then get a confirmation that your SQL query has been executed properly.

> ✔ Your SQL query has been executed successfully
>
> **DROP TABLE** `wp_commentmeta`,
> `wp_comments`,
> `wp_links`,
> `wp_options`,
> `wp_postmeta`,
> `wp_posts`,
> `wp_terms`,

[79]

Now, import the newly updated SQL file to your empty WordPress database as indicated in the screenshot below, and then click go.

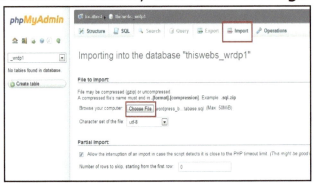

Upon importing the new SQL file, you should get a success message that your database has been successfully imported as indicated below.

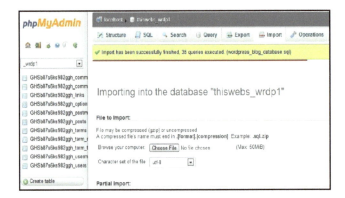

Open Up Wp-Config

The last piece of the puzzle is to edit wp-config.php. You should be able to find this file in the root directory of where you installed your blog.

Look for the code that states: $table_prefix ='wp_';

From there, replace the current table prefix with the new one you just made. Save and then exist out of your FTP software. The part of the code you should look for is highlighted in the screenshot below.

After this is done, you can activate your plugins and know additional peace of mind.

```
define('DB_HOST', 'localhost');

/** Database Charset to use in creating database tables. */
define('DB_CHARSET', 'utf8');

/** The Database Collate type. Don't change this if in doubt. */
define('DB_COLLATE', '');

/**#@+
 * Authentication Unique Keys and Salts.
 *
 * Change these to different unique phrases!
 * You can generate these using the [@link https://api.wordpress.org/secret-key/1.1/salt/ WordPress.org secret-k
 * You can change these at any point in time to invalidate all existing cookies. This will force all users to ha
 *
 * @since 2.6.0
 */
define('AUTH_KEY',         'Bj7ipQ1nR,yuuCw&uthiswebsiteisforeverything.infoAS-[%gQEpSr_=<dyb+>:Yd#nWbetyh~4ramMU
define('SECURE_AUTH_KEY',  '+fOIBXnJ~C{ftmT{[CA]]_wDSthiswebsiteisforeverything.infoG<K7#S8|H>/EaLy7]hijhRfj.K=
define('LOGGED_IN_KEY',    'c8K^-u_wU[BZ2ymK_sbOoI@?!thiswebsiteisforeverything.info}H< PM%7^l6VJTY.~DSOJ,zCEV7@
define('NONCE_KEY',        's5.9Yv+%:+HFX#l~ %RE AZ/pthiswebsiteisforeverything.infoUzn=&<R%7it-|[H~L+}AtN9/thn&
define('AUTH_SALT',        'KUEIq0~d.Tk<~t>1:HS95&G_^thiswebsiteisforeverything.infoZG,jcuq2}=7!#KE[~1c}Qw3a[LwG
define('SECURE_AUTH_SALT', ';OGoKVCGWIZh:YOa^h[]~T&Dithiswebsiteisforeverything.infonp=:iq;z$>OkEYN!2BY |5~c{n:}
define('LOGGED_IN_SALT',   'we3RP{hvolwbVh~{(L%LECHk!thiswebsiteisforeverything.info[IaA9<bDv1 h/M:3U7xK8S]A|.Q,
define('NONCE_SALT',       '~<M!ckLITB1GaIV)497^JDbe-}thiswebsiteisforeverything.infoG:^}/Prup?HeQMLNLzJkG~d/JO6X

/**#@-*/

/**
 * WordPress Database Table prefix.
 *
 * You can have multiple installations in one database if you give each a unique
 * prefix. Only numbers, letters, and underscores please!
 */
$table_prefix = 'wp_';
```

[82]

Security Plugins

One of the top security plugins that I would recommend for webmasters to utilize is iThemes Security (formerly Better WP Security). You can get it here: http://WordPress.org/extend/plugins/better-wp-security/.

The problem with WordPress plugins is without fully understanding the logic of the code; you are like a blind person being guided by a stranger. You have to put your full trust that the programmer made zero errors

[83]

and left zero vulnerabilities, which will only be seen once the plugin is exploited. However, I have reviewed the source code of the plugins that are about to be mentioned, and they do not contain any common programming exploits according to my

knowledge. So, in the worst-case scenario, make sure to backup all of your database information before installing any new WordPress plugin, whether it's free or commercial.

WordPress Plugin Installation Instructions

All plugins can be installed in one or two ways, so I'm going to show you once how to install plugins easily, and you can refer back to this whenever you forgot the steps.

Approach One

Log into your WordPress administrative control panel, and on the left-hand side of the screen, click on plugins, Add New, and then enter the plugin name, which is "iThemes Security." Click the "Search Plugins" button once done.

From there, click on the Install Now link as highlighted in the screenshot below.

Upon clicking this link, you should get a confirmation message that says "are you sure you want to install this plugin?" Click Ok.

[85]

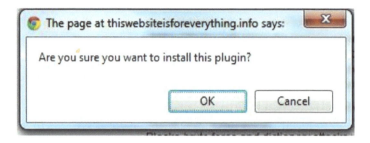

You should then get a confirmation that the package has been installed, but to use the plugin you must click "Activate Plugin."

Upon doing so, you should see Better WP Security listed under Plugins as indicated in the screenshot below.

Congrats, you have just installed a WordPress plugin.

The second approach

This approach is occasionally used if you were to install a commercial WordPress plugin or one that is not freely available in the WordPress repository.

Step One: Connect to your WebHost by using an FTP client like FileZilla: http://filezilla-project.org/. You need your hostname, username, and password to connect to your server. Contact your web host if you have never received these details.

Step Two: Download the plugin to your local machine. On every plugin page, there should be a download button that you can use.

Step Three: Extract the plugin so that it's no longer encapsulated within a .zip file.

Step Four: Upload the contents of the plugin to the path where your plugins are installed, which by default is: root/wpcontent/plugins.

Step Five: After the files have finished propagating login to your WordPress administrative control panel and then activate the plugin

Using iThemes Security (formerly Better WP Security)

Log in to your control panel, click on Plugins, and then click on settings for Better WP Security. Upon doing so, the plugin will ask you if you would like to backup your database. If you have already done so, then you don't need to, but if you haven't, then it's a good idea to go ahead and do this.

The next option is an exciting one. The plugin gives you two choices to automatically write to the core of WordPress using wp-config.php and .htaccess. As you know, I highly recommend you to do this yourself as if the plugin stop writing prematurely then your whole WordPress site may go offline, and you will have absolutely no idea where the issue is. However, if you're feeling ballsy and just don't want to do anything technical, then allow the plugin to

change WordPress core files. So after
selecting your option, you will be
presented with another dilemma,
which is to secure your site from
basic attacks or to configure

everything yourself.
I recommend to configure everything
yourself so that you have to know
what you are using the plugin for. As
I mentioned previously, never put
blind faith in something that you will
be using that affects your business as
that's wishful thinking.

Ban Users

Let's take a look at the Ban option, as
indicated in the screenshot below:

By selecting the Enable Default Banned List box, you'll be able to instantly blacklist IPs from bad neighborhoods in a heartbeat.

Hackers like to use proxies to scan websites for vulnerabilities so that they can be more difficult to track. You can make their lives much more difficult by not allowing commonly use proxies, which are included in the default blacklist.

Change The Wp-Directory

This option allows you to change the wp-content directory name of your WordPress site. Keep in mind that if you change the name of your wp-content on a live site with content uploaded there, then you will break your WordPress site.

In other words, this will only work if you have a fresh installation of WordPress without anything uploaded to it. If this is you, then rename the wp-content to any name you want as indicated in the screenshot below.

After doing this, click the Save Changes button and you are in business.

Hide WordPress Backend

Cloaking the URL of where you login as the administrator is a good idea as hackers know exactly where to go to to run a brute force attack on your WordPress site. For example, if your blog is installed on https://www.getpromoted.in/blog, then the path that I need to go to log in to the administrative control panel is www.getpromoted.in/blog/wp-admin.

Quick Quasi Hacker Experiment
Do you monitor any blogs online? If you do, then the chances are that the majority of them use WordPress. You can just view the source code and use ctr+f and scan for WordPress to see if there are any WordPress references in there. If so, then go to the wp-admin path on their server. If

you are paranoid, then you can use

A proxy to cloak your location, but remember you are just being nosey, and have zero intentions to actually crack into this site, or at least that's what I hope to believe. Do you see the username and password login options? If so then now you see why there are so many built-in vulnerabilities with WordPress, and to make matters worse, they are probably still using admin as their username!

Ok, so the main thing that we want to change is the admin login URL, so to do this simply highlight the "Enable Hide Backend" box, enter the new Admin Slug, and then click save as indicated in the screenshot below.

Hide Backend Options

Enable Hide Backend	☑
	Check this box to enable the hide backend.
Login Slug	login
	Login URL: http://thiswebsiteisforeverything.info/blog/login
Register Slug	register
	Register URL: http://thiswebsiteisforeverything.info/blog/register
Admin Slug	masterlock
	Admin URL: http://thiswebsiteisforeverything.info/blog/admin

Save Changes

Afterward, your old WordPress login of wp-admin will vanish, and you can log in to your administrative control panel by using your new admin slug.

Intrusion Detection

Click on the "Detect" tab in your WordPress admin panel. This feature allows webmasters to put constraints on users that have generated too many 404 errors. 404 errors happen when a user visits a non existing page on a site. If a user generates a lot of these errors in a short duration, then that would send off a red flag because they are data-mining a site for something, possibly a security weakness. So, enable the security features in this plugin, as shown in the screenshot below:

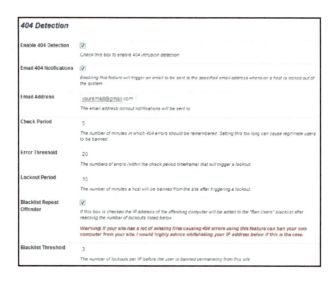

File Change Detection

If you scroll down in this section, then you should see another heading that says "File Change Detection." I would highly recommend enabling this option because if a WordPress file is changed without you being aware of it, then that is not a good sign. Click the *Enable File Change Detection* input box, as indicated in the

screenshot below.

Limit Login Attempts

Click on the Login tab within the plugin settings so that you can add some additional security to your WordPress login URLs. Say in the worst-case scenario, a hacker finds your new login page; they can still utilize the brute force attack to try and crack your password.

However, if you changed your username which you should have done earlier, and if you limit the number of login attempts they can make, then you will effectively stop them in their tracks. To limit the number of logins attempts that a user can make select the "Enable Login Limits" dialog box as indicated in the screenshot below.

It's pretty scary, but WordPress will allow a user to make infinite login attempts which is a terrible defense against a brute force attack, so this feature is a must-have.

Okay, this includes the features that I would recommend using with the better WordPress security plugin which shouldn't be painful at all. As always, I would recommend conducting further research to see if you can learn additional things.

Exploit Scanner

This is a nifty plugin that scans your WordPress database for possible threats and then notifies you of anything that seems fishy. It's a lightweight plugin that is useful and doesn't interfere with your WordPress site because it doesn't delete anything, just serves as a beacon for possible WordPress intrusions.

Here is the URL to download the plugin:

http://WordPress.org/extend/plugins/
[exploit-scanner/](http://WordPress.org/extend/plugins/exploit-scanner/). Once installed just run the scan as indicated in the screenshot below.

If you have cPanel, then it may be tempting to use an auto-installer like Fantastico or Softaculous to get your WordPress site up and running.

After all, in literally fifteen seconds, you can have a new WordPress site running perfectly. However, I would highly recommend against it or less you are using a website as a throwaway demo because there are some severe security vulnerabilities that you do not know about.

First, many scripts that are available via automated installers are outdated. Go ahead and install WordPress or any other opensource script via Fantasico, and you will see that most of them install previous versions of the scripts.

This is a big vulnerability because as explained earlier if an exploit is found in a previous version, then a hacker will have an easier time hacking into your site. Second, they provide template usernames for your WordPress databases, which is a big no-no, as explained earlier.

For example, your default WordPress database name after you installed WordPress via Fantasico would be wrdp1. Guess what the second database would be called, that's right wrdp2.

Can you guess the 150 one? Oh my, wrdp150, good golly you are right!

Those evil hackers will know the names of your databases if you are using an automated installer, and this gives them an extreme upside.

Third, the automated installers make your database username the same one as your database name! This again is a big no-no because all a hacker has to do use a brute force attack to crack my password! There is nothing else that they need to figure out.

Fourth, even though the database password does contain twelve characters, and a mixture of upper and lowercase letters plus numbers, I prefer some non-alphanumeric characters in there to make this more uncrackable.

Last, it creates a table prefix of wp_, which I discuss how to modify previously.

So I hope that I convinced you not to use those automatic installers for

WordPress sites that you plan to use for your business. I would highly recommend installing it from scratch so that you have control of the database name, user, and database prefix. Use the naming conventions I discussed previously to make your data much more secured.

Conclusion

Whether you finished reading this product, barely skimmed it, or too lazy to implement it, I want to highly convince you to implement all of these methods taught in this product day-by day. Set your schedule if you like, but just get it done because it needs to be. I hope you didn't misunderstand my intentions to scare you throughout this product because my sole intention was to scare the living daylights out of you so that you will take immediate action and start hardening your WordPress sites. Opensource technology is amazing, and there are tons of talented folks that contribute hours of code into making it more useful. However, it's simply naïve to think that there are no malicious users whose primary goal is to nuke someone's WordPress site and business from the face of the internet. If you think that it will never happen to you then I would invite you to wake up and smell the coffee, because the more your business grows, the higher chances is that it will get hacked if you ignore security.

Resources

Electronic Frontier Foundation:
https://www.eff.org/

Brute force attack:
http://en.wikipedia.org/wiki/Bruteforce_attack

How to become a hacker:
http://www.catb.org/esr/faqs/hackerhowto.html

Hackers for charity:
http://johnny.ihackstuff.com/category/projects/

Network protocol analyzer:
http://www.wireshark.org/

Https:
https://chrome.google.com/webstore/detail/usehttps/kbkgnojednemejclpggpnhlhlhkmfidi/details

www.ingramcontent.com/pod-product-compliance
Lightning Source LLC
Chambersburg PA
CBHW041152050326
40690CB00001B/444